An Overview of Utah Water Rights Law

Disclaimer

The information in this book is for informational purposes. It is inherently
general in nature, discusses the general rules, and does not discuss all exceptions. It is not a static interpretation of the law; the author and contributors
reserve the right to alter the statements herein. Case law and statutes may
change after this book is published. We will attempt to update this book to
include changes in the law. If you would like to receive updates, please send
us your email address at jschutz@mwjlaw.com.

This book is not intended as legal advice, and readers should consult with
legal counsel for advice relating to their specific factual situation. Using this
information or sending electronic mail to Mabey Wright & James, PLLC
or its attorneys does not create an attorney-client relationship with Mabey
Wright & James, PLLC.

An Overview of Utah Water Rights Law

JON SCHUTZ

With contributions from John Mabey, Jr., David Wright,
and Brooke Wangsgard of Mabey Wright & James, PLLC

www.mwjlaw.com

Author's Note

I immediately fell in love with water law during law school when I read *Cadillac Desert*. I am still enthralled by the history, politics, and conflicts associated with water use in the West.

When I first began practicing water law in Utah, I was hard-pressed to find a publication providing an overview of Utah water law. Some sources were too cursory; some were too lengthy and detailed. So I decided to write my own.

This publication is not meant to be an exhaustive discussion of the subject. In fact, it attempts to toe the line between being a thorough and accessible guide to water users and managers while not getting lost in the minutia of water law.

Opposition Creek, Colorado River headwaters.

"It is hard to be pessimistic about the West. This is the native home of hope. When it finally learns that cooperation, not rugged individuals, is the pattern that most characterizes and preserves it, then it will have achieved itself and outlived its origins. Then it has a chance to create a society to match its scenery."

– Wallace Stegner

TABLE OF CONTENTS

An Overview of Utah Water Rights Law

I. INTRODUCTION

"Irrigation in the United States, by Anglo-Saxon people, on a community scale, and under the conditions of modern civilization, began
in the Great Salt Lake Valley on July 24, 1847. On that day a company of pioneers under the leadership of Brigham Young, entered the
Valley with the purpose of settling and of building there a common-
wealth, and at once irrigated the land, plowed it, and planted potatoes
in the watered soil."[1]

Mormon settlers dammed City Creek in Salt Lake City in July
1847. The water was needed to soften the ground because "neither
wood nor iron were strong enough to make furrows in this hard soil."[2]
The Mormon pioneers were generally New Englanders who had
grown up in an area of plentiful rainfall, one where the riparian doctrine of water rights, based on land ownership abutting water, worked
well.[3] They quickly learned that in arid Utah, irrigation was required
because water was not located near the places where they wished to

---

[1] JOHN WIDSTOE, SUCCESS ON IRRIGATION PROJECTS 1 (1928).

[2] Leonard J. Arrington and Dean May, "A Different Mode of Life": Irrigation and Society in Nineteenth-Century Utah, 49 Agricultural History 7,
(January 1975), quoting Wilford Woodruff address at First National Irrigation Congress, Salt Lake City (1891).

[3] WIDSTOE, *supra* note 1, AT 2.

grow crops, and, as such, their riparian system of water rights would no longer be sufficient.[4]

Irrigation projects in Utah were cooperative endeavors. By 1865, Mormons "had dug, in Utah, 277 canals, 1044 miles in length; at a cost, including the cost of dams, of $1,766,959; by which 153,949 acres of land were irrigated…"[5]

Initially, LDS bishops organized the wards to dig canals and ditches within ward boundaries; once water was flowing, the bishops acted as water masters to regulate water distribution. Bishops also adjudicated water disputes. This introductory water rights administration system eventually gave way to a secular administration.[6]

In Utah, the public owns all the waters of the state.[7] An individual may obtain a water right to use the waters of the state. The Utah Division of Water Rights, administered by the Utah State Engineer, oversees the administration of water rights.

II.   UTAH HYDROLOGY

Utah is the second-driest state in the nation with 13 inches of average annual precipitation. Precipitation ranges from 50 inches in the high mountains to 5 inches in the deserts. After subtracting 3 million acre-feet (maf) of evaporation from the Great Salt Lake and 1 maf consumed by wetlands, Utah has about 3.3 maf of water each year for use by its residents.[8] Utah diverts about 5.15 maf and consumes about

---

[4]   *Id.* at 2–3.

[5]   *Id.* at 4; Arrington & May, supra note 2, at 8.

[6]   Arrington and May conclude that the Utah model of irrigation and irrigation institutions worked well in Utah, but could not serve well as a model for other communities that did not have the geographic advantages of the Salt Lake Valley (numerous mountain streams crossing the valley) and the social structure of a hierarchical church. ARRINGTON & MAY, *supra* note 2, at 19–20. They state that the Mormon irrigation success "derived more from the Mormon religious experience than from the ditch." *Id.*

[7]   Utah Code. Ann. § 73-1-1 (2000).

[8]   OFFICE OF LEG. RESEARCH & GEN. COUNSEL, HOW UTAH WATER WORKS: AN OVERVIEW OF SOURCES, USES, FUNDING, AND PRICING, 2–3

2.6 maf a year; some of that water is used more than once because of agricultural return flows.[9] Agriculture diverts 82% of the 5.15 maf, totaling 4.2 maf.[10]

III. PRIOR APPROPRIATION DOCTRINE

Water rights in Utah are governed under the prior appropriation doctrine.[11] The doctrine of prior appropriation arose from the physical reality of the arid West—water was not always located in the places people sought to use water. Water users had to move water from where it flowed to the desired place of use and ensure that other water users did not take the transported water. Therefore, the rule quickly arose allowing such transfers to the desired place of use; the water did not have to be used on lands adjacent to waterbodies, as required under the riparian doctrine. The doctrine was also to protect parties' investments in installing diversion works from later parties who could simply place a diversion upstream and take the water from the earlier water user.

In short, the prior appropriation doctrine is first in time, first in right. This means that the party who first establishes their water right has a superior claim and a higher priority over anyone who later diverts water from the same source.[12] For a water right established after 1903 through the permitting process described below, the priority is the date on which it was filed. For water rights established prior to 1903, the priority date is the date the water was diverted and put to beneficial use.[13] In times when there is not enough water for all the water rights from the source, the water right holder with the oldest

---

(Nov. 2012).

[9] *Id.* at 3-4.

[10] *Id.*

[11] In Utah, the appropriation doctrine prevailed even before Utah was a state and the riparian doctrine was never a part of Utah water law. *Stowell v. Johnson,* 26 P. 290, 291 (Utah 1891).

[12] Utah Code Ann. § 73-3-1(5).

[13] *See Elliott v. Whitmore,* 24 P. 673, 673 (Utah 1890).

water right (the water right first used historically) is called a senior water right holder and will be the last to have his water right curtailed.[14] The junior water right holders will have their right curtailed first and may lose all of their right before the senior water right holder will lose any of their right. In times of water shortage emergencies, water for drinking, sanitation, and fire suppression have a preferential right. Parties deprived of water during said emergencies are entitled to compensation.

IV. STATE ENGINEER'S OFFICE

The Utah State Engineer's office was created in 1897. The office was renamed the Division of Water Rights in 1963. The Division's stated mission is to "provide order and certainty in the beneficial use of Utah's water." The Governor, with consent of the Senate, appoints the State Engineer for a term of four years. The State Engineer is "responsible for the general administrative supervision of the waters of the state, and the measurement, appropriation, apportionment and distribution of those waters."[15]

The State Engineer may bring an action in court to "enjoin unlawful appropriation, diversion, and use" of water and to "prevent theft, waste, loss, or pollution."[16] The State Engineer may bring an enforcement action if it finds that a person (1) is diverting or using water to which they do not have a water right or in a manner that exceeds their water right, (2) violates a State Engineer order, or (3) fails to submit a required report. As part of its enforcement, the State Engineer may impose penalties: $5,000 for each knowing violation, $1,000 for each non-knowing violation, replacement of up to 200% of the water diverted, and the expenses incurred by the State Engineer in pursuing the violation.

---

[14] Utah Code Ann. § 73-3-21.1.

[15] *Id.* § 73-2-1.

[16] *Id.*

V. NATURE OF A WATER RIGHT

In Utah, and throughout most of the West, the right to use water beneficially is recognized as a valid property right. Under the Utah Real Estate code, "real property" or "real estate" includes "water rights... used, or enjoyed with the land or any part of the land."[17] But unlike a fee owner of real estate, a water right is unique in that the owner does not actually own the physical body of water. In fact, a Utah statute pronounces that "[a]ll waters in this state, whether above or underground are hereby declared to be the property of the public."[18] Thus, water right owners have only the right to use water under specified limitations—this right is referred to as a usufructuary right.

Because of this unique nature, a water right's value is its owner's ability to use it, its priority, and the ability to modify its use for another use. Like other property interests, a water right has different components that could be described as a bundle of rights, including the quantity, source, priority, place of use, nature of use, point of diversion, and period of use. As described herein, each of these characteristics is in the application to appropriate and may be modified via change application.

VI. OBTAINING A WATER RIGHT

In Utah's early history, one could acquire a water right by physically diverting the water and placing it to beneficial use. Some early statutory schemes allowed posting or recording notice of one's use, but did not preclude the method of establishing a right by diverting the water and placing it to beneficial use. Since 1903 for surface water and 1935 for groundwater, to acquire a water right in Utah one must follow the statutory permitting system.[19] One may also establish a

---

[17] *Id.* § 57-1-1(3).

[18] *Id.* § 73-1-1.

[19] *Id.* § 73-3-1(1).

water right by filing a diligence claim, as discussed herein.[20] One may not obtain a right through adverse possession.[21]

A. State Engineer's Permitting Process

Today one begins the process of obtaining a water right by submitting a form prepared by the State Engineer's office. A party may only seek a water right for "a useful and beneficial purpose." The State Engineer registers receipt of the application and then publishes notice of the application. "Any person interested" may protest the application. Only after the State Engineer approves a water right application may the applicant construct the works and apply the water to use.

The State Engineer must approve an application to appropriate water if there is reason to believe that:

(i) For an application to appropriate, there is unappropriated water in the proposed source;

(ii) The proposed use will not impair existing rights or interfere with the more beneficial use of water;

(iii) The proposed plan is physically and economically feasible, unless the application is filed by the Bureau of Reclamation, and would not prove detrimental to the public welfare;

(iv) The applicant has the financial ability to complete the proposed works;

(v) The application was filed in good faith and not for the purposes of speculation or monopoly; and

---

[20] *See Generally id.* § 73-5-13(outlining the procedure for filing a diligence claim). Diligence rights for water use prior to 1903 can be claimed according to statute by filing a diligence claim with the State Engineer. Certain underground water diversions established prior to 1935 are also a basis for a water right and those diligence claims, sometimes referred to as underground claims, may be filed at the office of the State Engineer. These diligence rights are those that predate statutory appropriative procedures.

[21] *Id.* §§ 73-3-1(6), 73-1-4(2)(d).

(vi) If applicable, the application complies with a groundwater management plan.[22]

If the State Engineer believes that the application will interfere with a water right's more beneficial use, "will unreasonably affect public recreation or the natural stream environment," or "will prove detrimental to the public welfare," the State Engineer must withhold approval or rejection until after he has investigated the matter. If the State Engineer approves the application, he must state the time by which the construction of the works must be completed and the water applied to beneficial use.

B. Diligence Claims[23]

A party claiming a right to water not based on a certificate of appropriation, an application filed with the State Engineer, or a court decree must file a diligence claim with the State Engineer. Practically, these claims usually involve water rights used prior to 1903 (surface water rights) and 1935 (groundwater rights). A diligence claim must be verified under oath by the claimant or their agent. The State Engineer has a designated form for diligence claims, requiring the claimant to include the quantity of water being claimed, the priority date, source of supply, point of diversion, place of use, and date of first use. The State Engineer may require additional information to evaluate the claims including affidavits, historic photographs, diaries, or personal histories.

Once a party submits a complete claim and money to pay for the expenses of conducting a field investigation, the State Engineer must file the claim, endorse the date the claim is received, assign the claim a water right number, and publish notice of the claim. The State Engineer's acceptance of the claim is not an adjudication of the claim's validity. The State Engineer must conduct a field investigation of each diligence claim filed and prepare a report of the investigation. The report becomes part of the claim's file and may be used in administrative or judicial proceedings regarding the validity of the claim.

---

[22] *Id.* § 73-3-8(1)(a).

[23] *See generally id.* § 73-5-13.

Any party damaged by use of water under the claim may bring an action in the district court to determine the validity of the claim in the county where the point of diversion or place of use is located. In such an action, the claimant has the burden of proof to establish the validity of the claim.

In a general adjudication, a district court may prohibit future diligence claims. If the State Engineer receives a diligence claim for an area where a court has prohibited future claims, the State Engineer must return the claim without acting on it.

Prior to May 1997, filing a diligence claim was considered prima facie evidence of a claim. Generally, diligence claims are not fully evaluated until someone files a change application on the claim that brings it before the State Engineer for consideration, a party files an action with the district court to determine the validity of the claim, or the claim is adjudicated as part of a general adjudication proceeding.

VII.   BENEFICIAL USE

"In Utah and other arid western states, 'a drop of water is a drop of gold.'"[24] Utah's "statutory and decisional law have been fashioned in recognition of the desirability and of the necessity of insuring... the most continuous beneficial use of all available water with as little waste as possible."[25]

To this end, all water rights may only be beneficially used. Stated differently, a water right holder may not waste water. Beneficial use is the basis, measure, and limit of a water right.[26] Even before beneficial use was codified, it was a requirement because "beneficial use 'has always been the basis of the right to appropriate and use waters in this

---

[24]   *Delta Canal Co. v. Frank Vincent Family Ranch, LC,* 2013 UT 69, ¶ 19, quoting *Carbon Canal Co. v. Sanpete Water Users Ass'n,* 425 P.2d 405, 407 (Utah 1967).

[25]   *Id.* ¶ 24, citing *Green River Canal Co. v. Thayn,* 2003 UT 50, ¶ 34, 84 P.3d 1134.

[26]   Utah Code § 71-1-3.

state.'"[27] Both the type of use and the amount of use must be beneficial. These requirements are ongoing requirements.

When one obtains a water right from the State, it is for a specified beneficial use. For example, a water right may be for the irrigation of five specific acres in a region with a four acre-foot (af) duty.[28] The duty is the maximum amount of water one may use in irrigating an acre of land. For example, in an area with a 4 af duty, one may apply up to 4 af per acre. In the example, the water right holder may divert up to twenty af for use on the designated five acres. The water right holder does not have twenty af for any uses he wishes: he may only use up to twenty af on the designated five acres. He cannot convert from flood irrigation to sprinkler, use thirteen af to irrigate the same five acres, and use the remaining seven af to irrigate new acreage. He also may not irrigate the specified five acres three days a week and another five acres the other four days of the week, nor while he harvests the designated five acres. Under current State Engineer policy, the irrigation water right is limited by the beneficial use of the authorized five acres.

VIII.   MODIFYING A WATER RIGHT: CHANGE APPLICATIONS AND EXCHANGE APPLICATIONS

A. Change Applications[29]

"A person entitled to the use of water" may temporarily (not more than a year) or permanently change the point of diversion, place of use, period of use, or the purpose of use of a water right from its original filing.[30] "A person entitled to the use of water" is "(1) the holder of an approved but unperfected application to appropriate water; (2)

---

[27]   *Delta Canal Co.*, 2013 UT 69, ¶ 19, citing *Sigurd City v. State*, 142 P.2d 154, 157 (Utah 1943).

[28]   The entire state is divided into irrigation duty areas—see map at Appendix A. Each area has a specified duty, ranging from three to six af per acre.

[29]   *See generally* Utah Code §§ 73-3-3 and 73-3-8.

[30]   *Id.* § 73-3-3.

the record owner of a perfected water right; (3) a person who has written authorization from a person…to file a change application on that person's behalf; or (4) a shareholder in a water company who is authorized to file a change application in accordance with Section 73-3-3.5."[31]

The change may not impair a vested right without compensation or adequate mitigation. A water right holder may only make a change after the State Engineer approves it; any change without approval will not create a right and is a criminal offense. To effect a change, the party must submit an application to the State Engineer on the prescribed forms, identifying the water right, quantity, source, present use, and proposed use.

The State Engineer's procedures in evaluating change applications, and an applicant's rights and duties in pursuing them, are the same as with applications to appropriate water. The change applicant has the burden, before the State Engineer "of producing sufficient evidence to support a reasonable belief that the change can be made in compliance with this section and Section 73-3-8."[32] This burden includes showing that the change will not cause "quantity impairment" to another water right and, if necessary, rebuts the presumption of quantity impairment if a portion of the water right has not been beneficially used at the approved place of use and not diverted from the authorized point of diversion for seven consecutive years.[33]

---

[31] *Id.* § 73-3-3(1)(b).

[32] *Id.* § 73-3-3(5).

[33] *Id.* §§ 73-3-3(5), 73-3-3(6)(c)(i). "'Quantity impairment' means any reduction in the amount of water a person is able to receive in order to satisfy an existing right to the use of water that would result from an action proposed in a change application, including: (A) diminishing the quantity of water in the source of supply for the existing right; (B) a change in the timing of availability of water from the source of supply for the existing right; or (C) enlarging the quantity of water depleted by the nature of the proposed use when compared with the nature of the currently approved use. 'Quantity impairment' does not mean a decrease in the static level of water in an underground basin or aquifer that would result from an action proposed to be taken in a change application, if the volume of water necessary to satisfy an existing right otherwise remains reasonably available." *Id.* § 73-3-3(1)(b).

The State Engineer must reject a permanent change application if the application cannot meet this burden.

However, the rebuttable presumption will not apply if the beneficial use is excused by an approved nonuse application or change application for instream flows, or if sufficient time has passed that a party is barred from challenging nonuse. It also does not apply in other situations such as when the source or priority of the water right does not yield water, the right is held by a public water supplier and is held for the reasonable future water requirement of the public, or the right is subject to an approved change application where the applicant is diligently pursuing certification.

Furthermore, the State Engineer may not consider quantity impairment under the presumption unless it is raised in a timely protest or by written notice of the State Engineer to the applicant within 90 days of the application being filed. This notice will go to the owners of the rights the State Engineer believes may be impaired by the proposed change. The owner of the right must file a protest to be a party in the administrative proceeding involving the change application.

In evaluating a change application, the State Engineer will evaluate historic diversion and depletion amounts and may limit the approved change to the historic depletion amount. This may reduce the volume of water diverted under the approved change from the historic diversion amount.

In approving a permanent or temporary change application, the State Engineer may impose the condition that the applicant acquire a conflicting right or that the applicant implement a plan to mitigate the impairment of an existing right. The State Engineer must approve the mitigation plan. Approval of a change application does not change the priority of the original application or extend the date when proof is due on the water right.

The State Engineer must investigate temporary change applications. If there is no reason to believe that the change will impair an existing right, the State Engineer shall approve the temporary change, but if the State Engineer finds there is reason to believe it will impair an existing right, he must deny the temporary change. A temporary change application may not be longer than a year.[34]

B. Change Applications for Instream Flows[35]

Instream flow protections are relatively recently in water law. Because a water right must be diverted and put to beneficial use, instream flow rights did not initially fit well into water law because they are not diverted and were not thought to be a beneficial use historically.

Now either the Division of Wildlife Resources or the Division of Parks and Recreation (a "Division") may file a permanent or temporary change application to provide instream flows in a specified section of a natural or altered stream channel to propagate fish, public recreation, or the preservation or enhancement of the stream environment. The change may be based on a perfected water right owned, purchased, or leased by a Division or an appurtenant water right attached to land a Division purchased.

A Division may only purchase a water right with funds specifically appropriated by the Legislature for the purchase of water rights. A Division may accept a donated water right. It may not condemn a water right.

A fishing group may file a change application for a fixed duration on a perfected, consumptive water right within a section of a natural or altered stream channel to protect or restore habitat for the Bonneville cutthroat trout, the Colorado River cutthroat trout, or the Yellowstone cutthroat trout. If the application is based on shares in a water company, the fishing group must follow the shareholder change application laws at Utah Code section 73-3-3.5, and the company must submit the application to a vote of its shareholders.

The section for the instream flow may not be upstream of the water right's original point of diversion or further downstream than the point of diversion by another person. The Division of Wildlife Resources' director must approve the fishing group's change application before it files the change with the State Engineer's office. The State Engineer will follow the same procedures on this application as

---

[34] *Id.* § 73-3-3(c).

[35] *See generally id.* § 73-3-30.

any application to appropriate water and the duties of the applicant for fish flows will be the same as any change applicant, including filing proof.

No party may file a new water right application to appropriate water for instream flows. The change for an instream right may not impair any vested water rights, including hydropower water rights. An approved instream flow application does not grant any right of access across private property.

C. Applications to appropriate or change a small amount of water[36]

The State Engineer may approve an application for a small amount of water if he undertakes an investigation of the application, determines the application complies with regional policies, and finds it does not conflict with local planning and zoning ordinances. A small amount of water is considered the amount of water necessary for one residence, 0.25 acres of irrigation, and a livestock water right for 10 cattle. The State Engineer has discretion on whether to advertise the application but must provide notice if he determines that the application may impair other water rights. A party may submit an affidavit as proof to obtain a certificate.

D. Exchange applications[37]

The State Engineer may approve exchange applications. Under the exchange application statute, a water right holder turns water from one channel into another channel or lake and co-mingles the water; a like quantity of water (minus evaporation and seepage) may be taken out at a point above or below the point where the water entered into the waterbody. The exchange may not deteriorate the quality of the original water or the quantity.

---

[36] *See generally id.* § 73-3-5.6.

[37] *Id.* § 73-3-20.

IX. PERFECTING A WATER RIGHT: FILING PROOF AND OBTAINING A CERTIFICATE

When the State Engineer approves a water right, he will prescribe the amount of time the water right holder has to perfect the water right—this is called the proof due date. Within this time period, the applicant must construct the works and put the water to beneficial use. The applicant must file proof with the state engineer with a description of the works, the quantity of water diverted, the method of use, and the measurement of water put to beneficial use. The proof must be sworn to.

Once the State Engineer is satisfied that a water right or change application has been perfected and put to beneficial use, the State Engineer grants a certificate stating the quantity of water, the purpose of use of the water, the time of use, the source, and the date of appropriation—the date of appropriation is the water right's the priority. A certificate is "prima facie evidence of the owner's right to use the water in the quantity, for the purpose, at the place, and during the time specified therein, subject to prior rights."[38]

If an applicant does not timely file proof or an extension request, the application will lapse. An applicant may request that the State Engineer reinstate the application. Within 60 days of the lapsing, the State Engineer may reinstate the application upon a showing of reasonable cause. If the State Engineer reinstates the application, it will have the priority date of the reinstatement.

Before the proof due date, an applicant may file a request to extend the proof due date. If the extension request is for a date more than 14 years after the original approval date, the State Engineer must publish notice of the extension request. A party who holds a water right from the same water source may protest the extension request. The State Engineer must extend the proof due date if the applicant shows reasonable and due diligence in completing the appropriation or reasonable cause for delay and the extended proof due date is within 50 years of the date on which the application was approved. A public water supplier holding a water right "to meet the reasonable

---

[38] *Id.* § 73-3-17(6).

future water…requirements of the public" will be considered to meet the reasonable and due diligence requirement for 50 years from the date the application was approved.[39]

If the applicant does not exercise reasonable and due diligence in perfecting the water right, the State Engineer may deny the extension or grant the extension with conditions, including a reduction in the water right's priority. With some exceptions, a party has 50 years to put their water right to beneficial use and file proof. For example, the State Engineer may extend the proof due date beyond 50 years if the applicant is a public water supplier and demonstrates that the water "is needed to meet the reasonable and future needs of the public."[40]

X. TRANSFERRING WATER RIGHTS BY DEED AND APPURTENANCE

Water rights are "transferred by deed in substantially the same manner as is real estate."[41] The deed must be recorded in the county recorder's office where the point of diversion is located and the county where the water is used. After July 2, 2011, a water rights deed may include a water rights addendum. The State Engineer will consider a water right addendum recorded in the county recorder's office and sent to the State Engineer as a report of conveyance to update the ownership records of the water rights.

Water rights appurtenant to land pass to a grantee of land unless the grantor:

1. specifically reserves the water right or any part of the water right in the land conveyance document;
2. conveys a part of the water right in the land conveyance document; or

---

[39] *Id.* § 73-3-12.

[40] *Id.* § 73-3-12.

[41] *Id.* § 73-1-10.

3. conveys the water right in a separate conveyance document prior to or contemporaneously with the execution of the land conveyance document.[42]

If the grantor conveys part of a water right in a land conveyance, it is presumed that the part of the water right not conveyed remains with the grantor. If the land conveyed is only part of the place of use of the water right, only the water right corresponding to the place of use is conveyed. For conveyances prior to May 4, 1998, if the water right has irrigated different parcels at different times, the water right will pass to the grantee of land on which the water right was used when the land was conveyed.

After May 4, 1998, the following water rights are appurtenant: (i) decree entered by a court; (ii) a certificated water right; (iii) a diligence claim for surface or underground water; (iv) a water user's claim executed for general determination of water rights proceedings; and (v) an approved application to appropriate, approved change application, or approved exchange application.[43] For land conveyances, the land to which a water right is appurtenant is the authorized place of use.

Shares of stock in an irrigation company are not considered water rights appurtenant to land. After May 14, 2013, shares will pass only as securities governed under the Uniform Commercial Code.

A water right holder may update the State Engineer's ownership records of the water right by submitting a report of conveyance (ROC) to the State Engineer. The State Engineer has a specific form for submitting the ROC. An attorney, professional engineer, title insurance producer, or professional land surveyor must prepare the reports.

---

[42] *Id.* § 73-1-11.

[43] *Id.*

XI. LOSS OF WATER RIGHTS[44]

When a water right holder ceases to use all or a portion of a water right for seven years, the unused portion is "subject to forfeiture."[45] A water right may not be forfeited unless "a judicial action to declare the right forfeited is commenced within 15 years from the end of the latest period of nonuse of at least seven years."[46]

In addition to case law defenses to forfeiture, forfeiture does not apply as defined by statute (1) to water that is leased; (2) to water that is unavailable because of its priority date; (3) to water that is unavailable because the source fails to produce adequate water; (4) to water that is stored in a reservoir or aquifer for present or future use; (5) to a water right where the water user has beneficially used substantially all of the water right within the seven-year period; (6) to a supplemental water right when another right is sufficient to cover the beneficial use and the supplemental water right is not needed; and (7) to a period of nonuse of a water right during the time the water right is subject to an approved change application and the applicant is diligently pursing certification.

The forfeiture statue does not apply to a water right (1) owned by a public water supplier; (2) represented by a public water supplier's interest in a water company; or (3) to which a public water supplier owns the right of use and is "conserved or held for the reasonable future water requirements of the public."[47] The "reasonable future water requirements of the public" are defined as "the amount of water needed in the next 40 years by: (A) the persons within the public water supplier's reasonably anticipated service area based on reasonably anticipated population growth; or (B) other water use demand."[48] For water rights acquired by a public water supplier after May 5, 2008, this section applies if the supplier submits a change application and the State Engineer approves the change application.

---

[44] *See generally id.* § 73-1-4.

[45] *Id.* § 73-1-4.

[46] *Id.* § 73-1-4(2)(c).

[47] *Id.* § 73-1-4(2)(e)(vii).

[48] *Id.* § 73-1-4(2)(f).

A public water supplier is defined as an entity that "supplies water, directly or indirectly, to the public for municipal, domestic, or industrial use."[49] The entity must be a public entity, a water corporation regulated by the Public Service Commission, or a community water system. If it is a community water system, the entity must supply at least 100 water service connections to year-round residents or regularly serve at least 200 year-round residents. The voting members "must own a share in the community water system; receive water from the community water system in proportion to the member's share in the community water system; and pay the rate set by the community water system based on the water the member receives."[50] A public water supplier also includes a water users' association "in which one or more public entities own at least 70% of the outstanding shares; and that is a local sponsor of a water project construction by the United States Bureau of Reclamation."[51]

If a water right is forfeited by judicial action, the water right reverts to the public. The forfeited water first satisfies other water rights in the hydrologic system and thereafter may be appropriated if available.

A party may file a nonuse application with the State Engineer on all or on a portion of a water right. If the application is approved, nonuse of the water during the approved nonuse period does not count toward the seven-year forfeiture period. Approval of a nonuse application does not protect a water right that is already subject to forfeiture. Any interested person may file a protest with the State Engineer against the nonuse application.

The State Engineer will grant the nonuse application for a period not exceeding seven years if the applicant shows reasonable cause for nonuse. Reasonable cause includes: "(i) a demonstrable financial hardship or economic depression; (ii) physical causes or changes that render use beyond the reasonable control of the water right owner so long as the water right owner acts with reasonable diligence to resume or restore the use; (iii) the initiation of water conservation

---

[49] *Id.* § 73-1-4(1)(b).

[50] *Id.* § 73-1-4(1)(b)(2)(C).

[51] *Id.* § 73-1-4(1)(b)(2)(D).

or efficiency practices, or the operation of a groundwater recharge recovery program approved by the state engineer; (iv) operation of legal proceedings; (v) the holding of a water right or stock in a mutual water company without use by any water supply entity to meet the reasonable future requirements of the public; (vi) situations where, in the opinion of the state engineer, the nonuse would assist in implementing an existing, approved water management plan; or (vii) the loss of capacity caused by deterioration of the water supply or delivery equipment if the applicant submits, with the application, a specific plan to resume full use of the water right by replacing, restoring, or improving the equipment."[52]

In a proposed determination, the State Engineer may not assert a water right is forfeited unless a seven-year nonuse period occurs during the fifteen years immediately preceding the State Engineer filing the proposed determination asserting forfeiture. After the proposed determination is filed with the court, no one may assert that the water right was forfeited during the preceding fifteen-year period unless the proposed determination asserts forfeiture, or if the party filed an objection to the proposed determination asserting forfeiture.

XII. CHALLENGING A STATE ENGINEER ORDER

A person "aggrieved" by an order of the State Engineer may file an action for judicial review under the Administrative Procedures Act (Utah Code Ann § 63G-4-101, et. seq.).[53] Venue for reviewing an informal State Engineer proceeding is the county in which the water source or a portion of the water source is located. The party filing the action must send written notice to each party who filed a protest in the State Engineer's action.

---

[52] *Id.* 73-1-4(4).

[53] *Id.* § 73-3-14.

XIII. IRRIGATION COMPANY ISSUES

A water company is "a corporation in which a shareholder has the right, based on the shareholder's shares, to receive a proportionate share of water delivered by the corporation."[54]

A. Shares

Each company shareholder is entitled to their proportionate share of water based on their shares in the company.[55] The Uniform Commercial Code governs the transfer of shares in an irrigation company. Most irrigation companies are nonprofit corporations organized under and governed by the Utah Nonprofit Corporation Act.[56]

B. Shareholder Change Applications[57]

A shareholder wishing to file a change application based on his shares in a water company must prepare the change application on the form provided by the State Engineer and provide the change application to the company by personal delivery with a signed receipt, certified mail, or electronic mail with confirmation of receipt. The change must also include the stock certificate number affected by the change, a description of the land to be retired from irrigation, if applicable, and an agreement wherein the shareholder agrees to pay all applicable assessments.

The company must respond to the application within 120 days in writing. The company may (1) approve the change; (2) approve the change subject to conditions; or (3) reject the change and describe the reasons for rejecting it. If the company does not respond within 120 days, the application will be deemed approved, and the shareholder may file it with the State Engineer.

In reviewing the change application, the company may consider:

---

[54] *Id.* §16-4-102; *see also id.* §73-3-3.5(1).

[55] *Yardley v. Long Canal Co.,* 177 P.2d 530, 531 (Utah 1947); *Baird v. Upper Canal Irr. Co.,* 257 P. 1060, 1065 (Utah 1927).

[56] *See generally Southam v. S. Despain Ditch Co.,* 2014 UT 35, 337 P.3d 236.

[57] *See generally* Utah Code §73-3-3.5.

1. Whether an increased cost to the water company or its shareholders results from the proposed change;
2. Whether the proposed change will interfere with the water company's ability to manage and distribute water for the benefit of all shareholders;
3. Whether the proposed change represents more water than the shareholder's proportionate share of the water company's right;
4. Whether the proposed change would create preferential access to use of particular company water rights to the detriment of other shareholders;
5. Whether the proposed change will impair the quantity or quality of water delivered to other shareholders under the existing water rights of the water company, including rights to carrier water;
6. Whether the proposed change violates a statute, ordinance, regulation, or order of a court or government agency;
7. If applicable, whether the shareholder has or can arrange for the beneficial use of water to be retired from irrigation within the water company's service area under the proposed change; and
8. The cumulative effects that the approval of the change application may have on other shareholders or water company operations.[58]

The company may not withhold its approval if any potential damage, liability, or impairment to the company or its shareholders can be mitigated without cost to the company. The company may require the shareholder to pay all the reasonable costs associated with the change application.

The shareholder may challenge the company's rejection of the application or its approval of the application with conditions in the district court.[59] The shareholder has a cause of action, including for

---

[58] *Id.* § 73-3-3.5(4).

[59] The court must refer the action to mediation and may award costs and reasonable attorneys fees to the prevailing party if mediation does not occur

actual damages, if the company unreasonably withholds approval of a requested change, imposes unreasonable conditions on the change, or inappropriately withdraws approval of the change. The court will review the reasonableness of the conditions imposed with approval or the reasons for rejecting the application. The court may award costs and reasonable attorney fees (1) to the shareholder if the water company acted in bad faith in declining to approve the change, or if it unreasonably conditioned it; or (2) to the company if the shareholder acted in bad faith in refusing to accept conditions reasonably necessary to protect other shareholders if the change was approved.

If the company approves the change subject to conditions, the shareholder may file the change with the State Engineer without waiving their right to contest the conditions in the district court. The shareholder may file the action during or after the proceeding before the State Engineer.

The shareholder may also file its change application with the State Engineer once the company consents to the change, consents with conditions, fails to respond within 120 days, or if a court has ruled on the conditions imposed by the company.

The application to the State Engineer must include the company's response to the change application, and, if applicable, an affidavit signed by the shareholder stating the company failed to respond within 120 days, as well as a court order resulting from the shareholder's challenge to the company's decision on the application. The State Engineer will evaluate shareholder change applications in the same manner it evaluates change applications under Utah Code sections 73-3-3 and 73-3-8.

Once the shareholder change application is approved, the shareholder may file extension requests without involvement from the water company. If the shareholder does not stay current on assessments, does not comply with conditions to approval of the change application, and fails to remedy the non-compliance after written notice from the company, the company may petition the State Engineer to reverse the change application approval after a 90-day notice.

---

because one party declines to mediate. *Id.* § 73-3-3.5(5).

It should be noted that a shareholder does not need to file a change application when they seek to divert water from a different point within the company's system.[60]

C. Company Management

The company's articles of incorporation "form the basis of a contract, among others, between the corporation and its stockholders...the provisions contained in the Constitution and statutes are as much a part of the articles of incorporation as though they were expressly copied therein."[61] Pursuant to the company's articles and bylaws, the company's Board of Directors is tasked with managing the affairs of the company and determining the best method for allocating the water to its shareholders.[62] As long as each shareholder receives their "fair share of the water...the court should not attempt to dictate the policy of the board of directors in solving the problem."[63]

D. Allocation of Water Lost by Forfeiture[64]

If part of an irrigation company's water right is lost due to forfeiture or abandonment, in whole or in part, the company will apportion the loss to each of the stockholders who caused the loss of the water right. The shares corresponding to the lost water right, including carrier water, shall be treated as treasury stock. In its records, the company must reduce the number of shares owned by the shareholder by the lost amount and the total number of shares in the company. The shareholder must still pay any assessments or debts owed on the shares.

---

[60] *Southam*, 2014 UT 35, ¶15 n.5, *citing Syrett v. Tropic & E. Fork Irr. Co.*, 89 P.2d 474, 475 (Utah 1939).

[61] *Fower v. Provo Bench Canal & Irr. Co.*, 101 P.2d 375, 376 (Utah 1940); *see also Salt Lake City v. Cahoon Irr. Co.*, 879 P.2d 248, 252 (Utah 1994).

[62] Utah Code §§ 16-6a-611, -801(20)(a); *Yardley*, 177 P.2d at 531.

[63] *Yardley*, 177 P.2d at 531; *Fower*, 101 P.2d at 379.

[64] *See generally* Utah Code § 73-3-4.5(1).

XIV. GENERAL ADJUDICATIONS

A general adjudication is a court action to determine all of the water rights on a given water system. Five or more (or a majority) of water users on a water source may petition the State Engineer to investigate all the water rights in the source. The State Engineer will investigate and determine whether a general adjunction is appropriate and, if so, file an action in the district court for a general adjudication of the water rights.

The State Engineer must locate "all possible claimants" and give notice of the commencement of the action to all claimants by pub-lishing notice and serving them a summons.[65] After publishing notice of commencing the general adjudication, the State Engineer must begin surveying the "water sources and the ditches, canals, wells, tunnels and other works diverting water from the water source."[66] Once the survey is complete, the State Engineer notifies all claim-ants. Within 90 days of the notice of the completed survey, any claim-ant claiming a water right must submit a claim statement. Any per-son not making a claim within 90 days "shall be forever barred and estopped from subsequently asserting any rights, and shall be held to have forfeited all right to the use of water."[67] However, if a party received notice by publication, they may petition the court for addi-tional time to file a claim, and the court may grant up to six months from the time notice was published. The court may also allow parties to amend their claims; may "extend as provided in this title the time for filing any statement of claim; and extend, upon due cause shown, the time for filing any other pleading, statement, report or protest."[68]

After considering all the claims and its own investigations, the State Engineer must formulate a report and a proposed determina-tion (PD) of all rights to the use of the river system or source. The State Engineer must serve notice of the completion of the report and PD on all claimants, including a copy of the PD. Any claimant may

---

[65] *Id.* § 73-4-3.

[66] *Id.*

[67] *Id.* § 73-4-9.

[68] *Id.* § 73-4-10.

file an objection to the PD within 90 days of receiving notice of completion of the PD. If the objection is not heard promptly, any claimant to the use of water may petition the court to expedite a hearing on timely objections in which the claimant has a direct interest.

The State Engineer shall distribute the waters at issue in accordance with the PD until the court enters a final decree. If the court has already entered a decree for the waters at issue in the PD, the State Engineer shall distribute the waters in accordance with the decree until it is modified, reversed, or vacated. If no party files an objection, the court shall adopt an order conforming to the PD. The statement of claims filed will serve in the place of legal pleadings. Whenever requested by the court, the State Engineer will furnish the court with any information he possesses. After hearing the objections, the court will enter an order that "will fully and completely define the rights" of the claimants to the use of water.[69] The district's court order may be appealed.

XV. WATER RIGHT OWNER PRIVILEGES

Any person has a right of way across public or private lands for the construction, maintenance, repair, and use of all necessary reservoirs, dams, water gates, canals, ditches flumes, and pipelines for securing, storing, and conveying water for domestic, culinary, industrial, and irrigation use, or for drainage upon compensation to the impacted property owner. The condemned right of way must be "exercised in a manner not unnecessarily to impair the practical use of any other right of way, highway, or public or private road, or to injury any public or private property."[70]

When a person without an interest in a canal or ditch wishes to convey water for irrigation or another beneficial use, and there is a canal or ditch constructed that could be used or enlarged to convey the water, the person may use or enlarge the ditch if: (1) the ditch or canal can be used without displacing current users and exceeding free

---

[69] *Id.* §§ 73-4-12, 73-4-15.

[70] *Id.* § 73-1-6.

board capacity or enlarged to convey the water to carry current users' water, maintain free board capacity, and convey the additional water; and (2) the person compensates the owner of the ditch or canal for any damage caused, as well as each landowner whose land is encumbered by the ditch or canal's easement if the carrying of additional water expands the easement's scope.[71] This privilege applies only to canals and ditches and not any other type of infrastructure.

The enlargement must occur between October 1 and March 1 unless the owner of the canal or ditch and the encumbered landowners agree otherwise. The new water in the canal or ditch must take seepage losses into account.

Before any use or enlargement occurs, including any condemnation for such use under Utah Code section 73-1-6, the person seeking to use the canal or ditch must negotiate in good faith with the canal owner and the landowners encumbered by the canal to enter into a written agreement concerning the use or enlargement.

By using the existing the canal, the new party

1. Does not acquire any voting rights in the entity owning the canal or ditch not already possessed;
2. Does not acquire any rights to direct the operation of the canal or ditch;
3. May not add water to the canal or ditch that impairs the water quality in the canal or ditch or increases the cost of any treatment to a degree that adversely impacts the intended use of the water already in the canal or ditch;
4. May not add water to the canal or ditch that exceeds the capacity of the canal or ditch, including free board capacity;
5. May not modify any water rights without state engineer approval;
6. Shall pay an equitable proportion of construction or upgrade costs, including any related debt service incurred by the owner of the canal or ditch within five years before the day on which the person begins use of the existing canal or ditch;

---

[71] *Id.* § 73-1-7(1).

7. Is liable for an equitable proportion of any liability arising out of the operation or maintenance of the canal or ditch unless the event giving rise to the liability was caused solely by the person or by the owner of the canal or ditch;

8. Is solely liable for any liability arising out of the operation or maintenance of the canal or ditch if the event giving rise to the liability was caused solely by the person; and

9. Is not liable for any liability arising out of the operation or maintenance of the canal or ditch if the event giving rise to the liability was caused solely by the owner of the canal or ditch.[72]

When two or more people are associated to use a reservoir, dam, canal, ditch, lateral, or other means of conveying or conserving water, each person is liable to the other for reasonable expense of maintaining and operating it in proportion to their use or ownership of the water.

When a party diverts water, they may use and reuse the water as long as they maintain control over it.[73] Another water user is not entitled to the return flow and cannot compel its release until the original water user relinquishes control of the water and returns it to the natural system; only then it is subject to appropriation by another party.[74]

XVI. CRIMINAL ACTS AFFECTING WATER RIGHTS

It is a criminal offense for any person to interfere with, injure, destroy, or remove any structure or device for diverting apportioning, measuring, or regulating water, including a dam, head gate, weir, or valve.[75] It is also a criminal offense to interfere with any person authorized to apportion water while that person is performing their duties. A

---

[72] *Id.* § 73-1-7(6).

[73] *Estate of Steed v. New Escalante Irr. Co.*, 846 P.2d 1223, 1225 (Utah 1992).

[74] *Id.*

[75] Utah Code § 73-1-14.

person committing such an offense is also liable in a civil action for damages.

Vested rights in established canals and watercourses are to be protected against all encroachments. It is a criminal offense to place or maintain any obstruction or change of the water flow along, across, or in an established canal right of way (except where it damages private property) without first receiving written permission for the change. The obstructing party must also provide gates sufficient for the owners of the canal or watercourse to pass the obstruction.

It is also illegal to engage in well drilling without a license to do so.[76] A person may not make a temporary or permanent change without first obtaining approval for the change from the State Engineer.[77] A person may not "knowingly or intentionally relocate a natural stream channel, or alter the bed or bank of a natural stream channel without first obtaining written approval of the State Engineer."[78]

> No person may knowingly or intentionally:
>
> Turn or use the water, or any part thereof, of any canal, ditch, pipeline, or reservoir, except at a time when the use of the water has been duly distributed to the person;
>
> Use any greater quantity of the water than has been duly distributed to him;
>
> In any way change the flow of water when lawfully distributed for irrigation or other useful purposes, except when duly authorized to make the change; or
>
> Break or injure any dam, canal, pipeline, watergate, ditch, or other means of diverting or conveying water for irrigation or other useful purposes.[79]

---

[76] *Id.* § 73-3-26.

[77] *Id.* § 73-3-3(7).

[78] *Id.* § 73-3-29.

[79] *Id.* §76-10-202(1).

This applies to violations "of any right to the use of water," including a water right or water taken out of turn in an irrigation company.

Each of these violations is punishable
1. As a third degree felony if:
    a. The value of the water diverted or property damaged or taken is $2,500 or greater; and
    b. The person violating the provision has previously been convicted of violating the same provision;
2. As a class A misdemeanor if:
    a. The value of the water diverted or property damaged or taken is $2,500 or greater; or
    b. The person violating the provision has previously been convicted of violating the same provision; or
3. As a class B misdemeanor if neither of the preceding two circumstances apply.[80]

---

[80] *Id.* §73-2-27.

Appendix A

State Engineers since statehood

1. Willard Young 1897 – 1898
2. Robert C. Gemmell 1898 – 1901
3. A.F. Doremus 1901 – 1905
4. Caleb Tanner 1905 – 1913
5. W.D. Beers 1913 – 1917
6. G.F. McGonagle 1917 – 1921
7. R.E. Caldwell 1921 – 1924
8. Lloyd Garrison 1924 – 1925
9. George M. Bacon 1925 – 1933
10. T.H. Humphreys 1933 – 1941
11. Ed H. Watson 1941 – 1949
12. Harold A. Linke 1949 – 1950
13. Joseph M. Tracy 1950 – 1957
14. Wayne D. Criddle 1957 – 1965
15. Hubert C. Lambert 1965 – 1973
16. Dee C. Hansen 1973 – 1985
17. Robert L. Morgan 1985 – 2002
18. Jerry D. Olds 2002 – 2008
19. Kent L. Jones 2009 – Present

Appendix B

Images

Construction of the Strawberry Project, ca 1902. Visionary Utah settlers realized the importance of large scale water supply projects that could capture Colorado River water.

A typical method for transporting pipes in the early 1900s.

Construction of Deer
Creek Dam, ca 1941.

JVWCD

Deer Creek Reservoir, 2008.

A South Jordan farm, ca 1950, shows irrigation methods
still used many years after Utah settlers arrived.

Construction of water transporting tunnels such as the Duchesne
Tunnel, shown here, was often dangerous work.

The completed Duchesne Tunnel
transports water from the Duchesne
River to the upper Provo River.

Installing "Reach 2" of the Jordan Aqueduct, 1972.

Construction of Jordanelle Dam, 1986 - 1993. Water stored in Jordanelle Reservoir provides drinking water to the Salt Lake Valley and is essential during times of draught.

High Uintah lakes are one of many sources used for drinking water. Water from lakes such as this one must travel great distances before being treated and used.

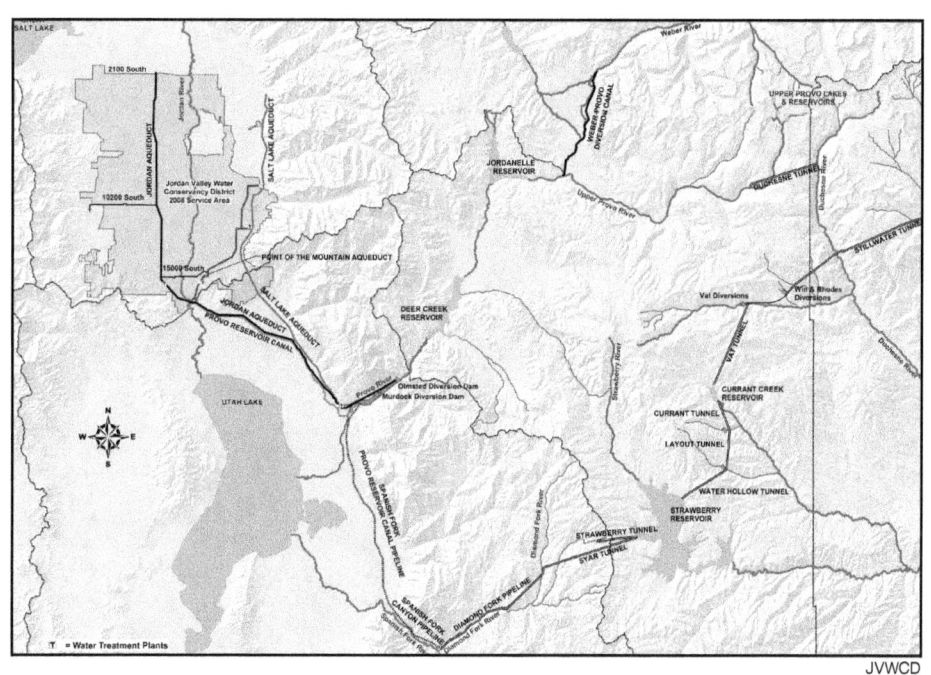

Getting water to the Salt Lake Valley requires hundreds of miles of water delivery systems and coordination among several agencies. This map shows part of the Central Utah Project, the largest of several Utah water-management and supply projects.

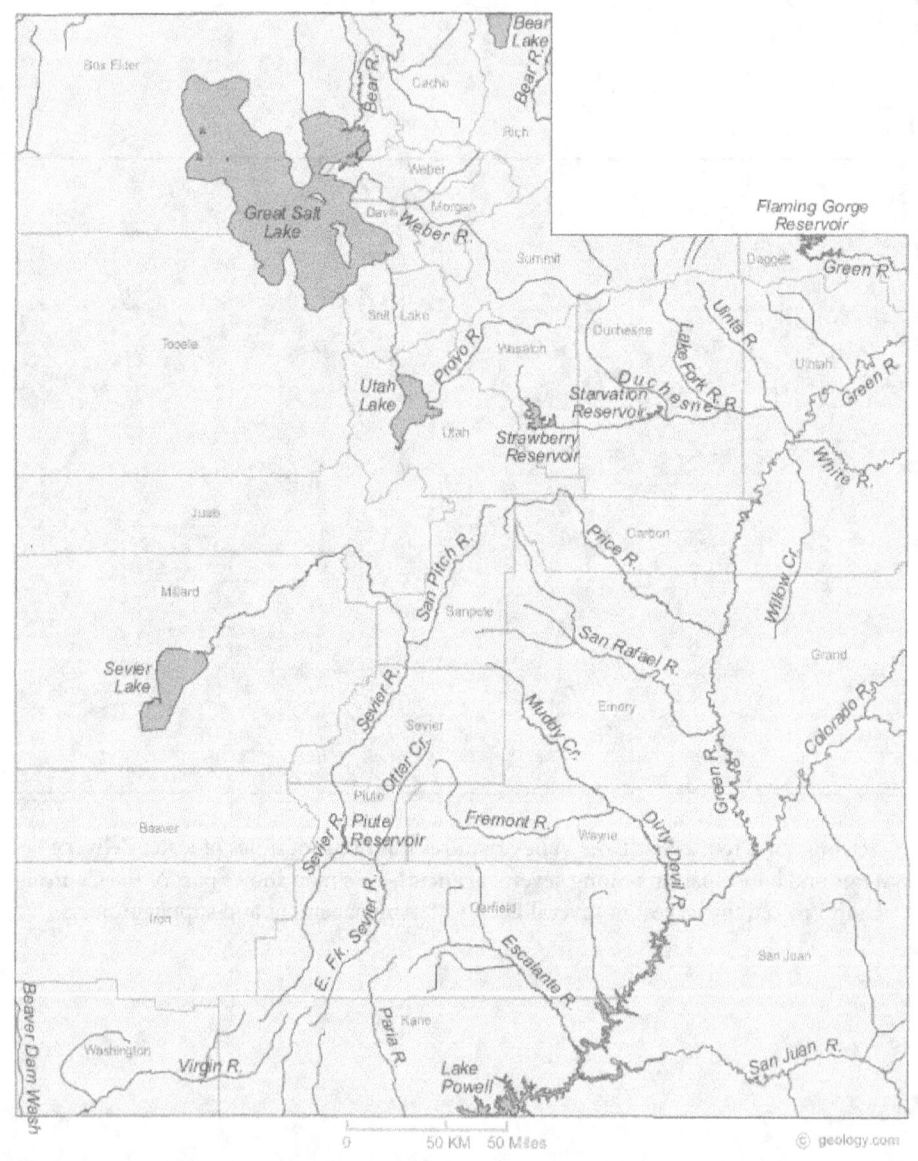

Utah's major river systems

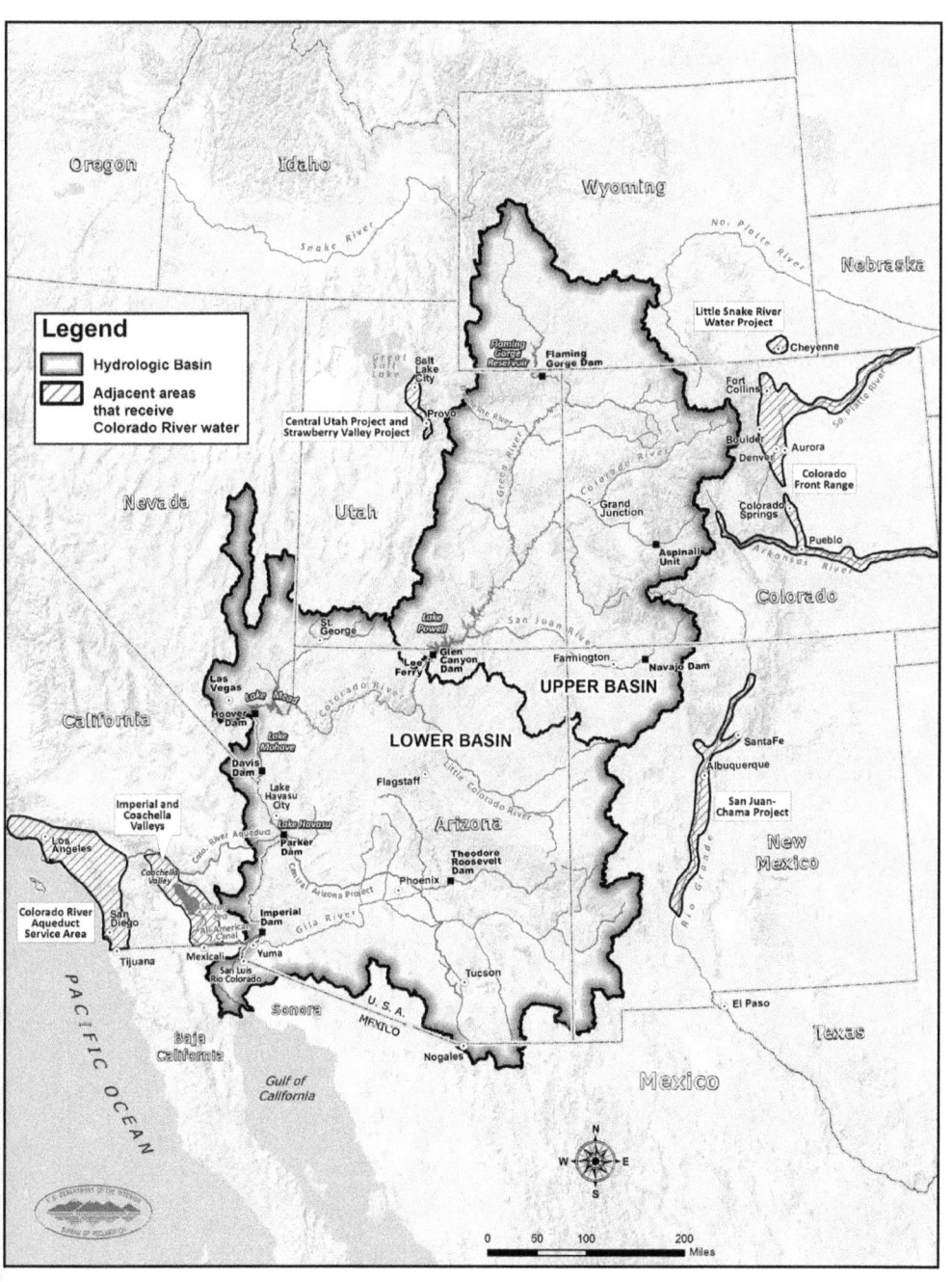

Colorado River watershed

About Mabey Wright & James, PLLC

Mabey Wright & James (MWJ) is a Salt Lake City, Utah law firm offering legal services in the areas of water law, environmental law, commercial litigation, general business, and employment law. The firm is recognized in Best Law Firms for water law by U.S. News and World Report.

In the area of water law, MWJ regularly handles all manner of water right matters, including water right evaluations, due diligence, general adjudications, change applications and other permits; water rights purchase transactions; and water right title updates. MWJ has extensive litigation experience and success in each of these areas. In environmental law, MWJ assists clients to comply with National Environmental Policy Act (NEPA) and the endangered species act and obtain Clean Water Act section 404 wetlands permits. MWJ represents cities and other public water suppliers, irrigation companies, mining and industrial companies, public utilities, and various business and development interests.

MWJ assists clients in the following employment law matters: Federal Court litigation, contracts, employment confidentiality and non-compete agreements, discrimination, harassment, ADA, FMLA, manuals, training and claim prevention.

MWJ also assists clients in state and federal court litigation in water rights, real property, commercial contracts, partnerships, eminent domain, employment, construction and corporate governance.

www.mwjlaw.com

Disclaimer

The information in this book is for informational purposes only. It is not a static interpretation of the law; the author and contributors reserve the right to alter the statements herein. We will attempt to update this book to include changes in the law. If you would like to receive updates, please send us your email address at jschutz@mwjlaw.com.

It is not a substitute for legal advice applying the law to specific facts, and readers should consult with legal counsel for specific advice. In addition, using this information or sending electronic mail to Mabey Wright & James, PLLC or its attorneys does not create an attorney-client relationship with Mabey Wright & James, PLLC.